7 FOUNDATIONS
OF
Health and Happiness

Building a Bridge to Balance

7 Foundations of Health and Happiness: Building a Bridge to Balance

This work is licensed under a Creative Commons Attribution-NonCommercial-ShareAlike 3.0 Unported License. You may share or build upon any part of this work for non-commercial purposes, as long as you include the following attribution:

Copyright © 2013 Chanel Heermann, SynerGenius Consulting, Denver, Colorado
info@synergeniusconsulting.com; 720-515-1315; www.synergeniusconsulting.com

Cover and interior design by Jamie Runyan

www.reese-winslow.com

Published by SynerGenius Publishing,
an imprint of The Publishing Consortium, LLC

For Travis and Kaya, who have supported and inspired me

to become the person I am today,

and without whose love and understanding

this book would not exist.

7 FOUNDATIONS OF *Health and Happiness*

Building a Bridge to Balance

CHANEL HEERMANN MD

How to Use This Book

This workbook was created to support you in assessing your current life balance in seven key areas, so you can begin to create the life you truly want. In order to move forward, you need to really know where you are right now. These questions are key to understanding your situation – what's holding you back, and where you want to go. I urge you to make a plan to begin working on the exercises right away, before your obligations have a chance to put this on the back burner and, once again, get in the way of building your happier life.

If you have reviewed *7 Foundations of Health and Happiness: First Steps* previously, you will notice the addition here of the "Going Further" section in each Foundation. The purpose of the "Going Further" section is to deepen your understanding of your life in the area of each Foundation, and to offer opportunities to explore other important areas that were not covered fully in the "First Steps" questions. This workbook also contains additional exercises designed to bring everything together into a "big picture" of your life and goals, as well as helpful information on implementing your new insights in your everyday life.

If you have recently completed the *7 Foundations of Health and Happiness: First Steps* exercises, you don't need to complete the "First Steps" section again. Simply begin with the "Going Further" section in each Foundation. However, if it has been awhile since you first explored these questions, you may find it beneficial to answer them again, to see how far you've come and if anything in your life has shifted for you since you last answered them.

I find that I think best if I give myself a block of time to really reflect and go deep into the process. I suggest blocking out two hours when you won't be interrupted – perhaps first thing in the morning, or after the kids are in bed, or maybe on a free weekend afternoon. You may find it takes a couple of time blocks to get it done – that's fine, too. I have had also good experiences with blocking out a weekly lunch hour to work on my own self-reflection. It doesn't matter when – just find a time that fits for you. The key, though, is to make the time!

Some people like to really immerse themselves in this process, and work through all the questions together as part of a weekend retreat or other personal reflection time. Others find it easier to process the learning in smaller pieces, so feel free to review one Foundation at a time, if you prefer. People just starting out with the 7 *Foundations* process sometimes find it easier to complete the First Steps for all seven Foundations, and then return later to the "Going Further" section to explore each Foundation more deeply. Whatever order seems to fit for you is the "right" way to explore this resource.

As you are completing each question, remember to reflect without judging yourself. Know that you are doing the best you can, with the resources you have, at this moment. There is no right or wrong answer. Rather, this is a learning process – to learn more about your life, as it is right now.

Before beginning this workbook, some people find it helpful to set an intention for your work. For example: Why are you choosing to spend time exploring your life with this workbook? What would you like to change or improve in your life as a result of your work here? What are your expectations and hopes for this process? What do you wish to learn?

If you like, take a moment to write down your intention for this process here:

Notes:

Introduction

So how have you found yourself with this book in hand?

Chances are, you are a take-charge, no-nonsense professional – a go-getter who has been successful in many areas of your life. You have the career, you have relationships with friends, maybe a partner, and perhaps you even have children. You have achieved a lot.

But perhaps your prior achievements only make it that much harder for you to understand your current difficulties in balancing career, family, and having a life of your own.

If the thought of "What life?" has crossed your mind, you're in the right place.

You've done everything "right" for so long that it's nearly impossible to comprehend why something, right now, is very wrong. So many professionals feel just like you do. The temptation, especially if you're a perfectionist like me, is to blame yourself.

But it's not your fault.

The problem is stress – constant, unmanageable, life-sucking stress. Doubtless you have heard this before, in other places, throughout your life, but stress is so easy to forget in the chaos of daily life.

The overwhelming stress many of us experience means we are less effective in all areas of our lives.

At work, this loss of effectiveness means you have less ability to produce in accordance with your talents, which also likely means less income, less respect from others for the quality of your contribution, and less ability to engage in community with other professionals. More importantly, when you're overwhelmed, it's impossible to work in integrity with your highest values, or to really receive the enjoyment and satisfaction you deserve.

Even more disturbing is the effect of stress on our relationships. We simply have fewer resources available to connect deeply with those we love. Are you often aware, in the sea of competing demands for your time, of a feeling that you're neglecting someone or something? Over the long-term, this increased stress and conflict can lead to breakdowns of significant relationships, such as divorce or estrangement from loved ones. However, even if the relationships survive our distraction, we are guaranteed to get less enjoyment from them than we long for.

When this level of stress goes on long enough, it dramatically impacts our health and well-being. We develop chronic illness and psychological symptoms, and our risk of serious illness skyrockets. Even if we aren't yet seeing overt illness or disability, we have less energy and vitality, and experience less enjoyment of life. Our lives simply feel out of control. We are too stressed to make choices in line with our values and fall back into convenient routines, too busy to really evaluate use of resources and how they support our big goals.

So the real question becomes: if what you're doing isn't making you happy – why are you still doing it?

A Quick Checklist for Life Change Readiness

Are you...

- Stressed out, exhausted, and buried under your many responsibilities?

- Wondering why, despite all your success, your life simply feels out of control?

- Feeling overwhelmed, too busy to really reflect on what you want out of life?

- Exhausted, burned out, and lacking the energy to do things you enjoy most, things that are meaningful and important? Like time to connect with your partner? Playtime with your kids? Time to curl up with a good book, or to go for a walk?

- Tired of ignoring that nagging feeling of disconnect – from the causes you care about, from the people you love most ... even from yourself?

If you answered "yes!" to any of the above, let me congratulate you on taking the first step in making a change in your life. This book can be the beginning of a wonderful new journey.

The first step to making choices that are truly aligned with our values is to examine and accept where we are right now. Sometimes this is the hardest part – taking a fearless look at the choices we are making now, and noticing any patterns that aren't serving us anymore.

Be gentle with yourself in this process. Know that you are doing the best you can, and that anytime you have said "no" to something important, it is because you are saying "yes" to something that feels like the most important thing in that moment.

Making new choices can be a little scary. We all have old familiar patterns, comfortable ways of doing things, but sometimes those old patterns don't fit for us anymore, even when we can't quite put our finger on why.

Building new, more beneficial patterns is what this book is about.

My Story

I used to feel this fear of change, trusting that the way I had always done things would always be fine. I used to engage in the same self-defeating behaviors that are the foundation for a life that is out of balance and, frankly, out of control. Instead of controlling my stress, I was controlled by stress, unable to create a life I loved, the kind of life I longed for, bouncing back and forth between dozens of unfinished and, often, unimportant projects, always feeling like the charade could collapse at any moment. I spent years on that perfectionistic hamster wheel. The scariest part was that, despite my constant activity, I never felt like what I did was enough – like I was enough.

The birth of my daughter should have been a call to re-prioritize my life and eliminate some things to make room for this new person in my life. Instead, I simply added mothering to the top of all the other things I had to do. When I spent time rightfully focusing on my new baby, I felt guilty for neglecting my career, for not being a "good enough" feminist, for somehow not doing enough to create a world where my daughter could "have it all".

I'm not sure why I thought the best way to build that world was to run myself into the ground.

It's funny – I would never have wanted my child to live a life so out-of-balance, so exhausted, so sleep-deprived, and so wrapped up in frantic activity, living in terror that the slightest misstep will cause the whole house of cards to come crashing down on her.

And yet, I didn't think twice about doing that to myself.

A few years ago, I had just moved to a new city, in a new state, away from all my old friends. I had taken a new job, where I soon discovered that the position was not as advertised. Couple these issues with a difficult boss and a long commute, and I was on the fast track to crash. I simply ignored my body's early warning signals, so crash I did. I suppose the first time I ended up in the hospital should have been a wake-up call.

And it was ... for a little while. But, pretty soon, I fell back into my old bad habits.

Until it happened again, two years later. I joked at the time that the best way to get a few unquestioned days off was to actually collapse at work. After all, if they have to call the EMTs to come fetch you, surely that should buy you a couple days off to ignore your emails. But it was no joking matter.

As I lay in the hospital, I knew deep down that I needed to make a change, that my life depended on it. If I didn't do something to rein in my destructive perfectionism and chronic stress I was going to end up chronically, seriously ill, or worse.

The irony is that I had been studying integrative medicine, holistic medicine, and mind-body medicine for years. I had even been trained in compassionate communication and positive psychology – but none of that seemed to make much difference in how I lived my life, in the choices I made. What I needed most was to apply those years of training and practice with others to myself first – to allow my knowledge to make that long, 18-inch trek from my head to my heart, so that I could start living these skills.

And I did.

By synergizing all the things I have learned over many years of study, combined with scientifically based techniques for making my changes "stick", I have been able to synergize the best of science and wisdom into a system that changed my life, and the lives of those around me.

However, memories of my own out-of-balance, chaotic, unhappy life are a constant reminder of how far I have come. Back then, I didn't want to answer the hard questions. I didn't truly want to figure out the source of my uneasy feeling that something just wasn't right, even though at certain moments I realized I was wasting my one precious life. It would have been so easy to just keep plugging along and ignoring that little voice in my head, telling me something desperately needed to change. At least, it would have been easier in the short run.

I'm not in this to build an amazing life in the short run, however. My goal is to continue building a life that sustains and fulfills me, connecting me to my own higher purpose. And, I want that for you, too.

For that reason, I created this book.

Your Story

Is the time right for you to change your own story? Are you ready and willing to make the small changes you need to change the course of your life? Isn't it time to find out?

This workbook is filled with the kind of important questions you've likely been avoiding asking yourself – the important questions you must answer if you want to create the life you've always longed for. Based on these questions, you will complete three crucial exercises that will allow you to see visually where you are right now, to explore any unrealistic expectations, and to clarify what balance would look like for you.

I regularly use these questions to look at my own life – fearlessly, with authenticity, and with compassion – to see where I might want to shift or grow to make my path even happier.

You, too, can build a life you love – a life that truly makes you happy.

Consider this process a roadmap to the life you want. First, before you can begin your journey, you must know exactly where you are. Come with me and let's take this first step together.

As you answer the questions in this workbook, take time and reflect on your answers. Take a few deep breaths between answers and let your inner knowing help you to give the most honest answer you can, to the most important person in your life – yourself. Consider your past – times when you have been successful before. Consider your future – how you hope to grow and change. But most of all, just be present with what is, right now, for you, in your one precious life.

This is YOUR journey, your story. Let's get started!

Rest

INCLUDING RELAXATION, SLEEP, STRESSORS, AND PLAY/RECREATION

Foundation 1 encompasses all that you do to rejuvenate yourself. This includes everything from your relaxation practices and stress management, to sleep habits, to how you play.

Answer the questions below about this important area of your life. Take your time and really reflect on your answers.

First Steps

1. What has been stressing you out lately?

2. How much sleep do you get? What is its quality?

3. Do you take the time to relax for at least a few minutes a day?

4. Do you have regular time set aside for recreation or play?

5. Do you have the high energy you need to do what you want?

Going Further

1. Think of your biggest current stressor. What situations like this one have you effectively dealt with in the past?

2. How many days a week do you awaken in the morning feeling well rested and energetic, with more than enough energy to meet your daily responsibilities? Why do you think that is?

3. Do you explore the symbolism and emotional content of your dreams? If so, any recent themes or patterns?

4. Do you get enough rest during your day? When and how does that happen?

5. Do you do any regular relaxation practices? If so, what kind and how often? Does that feel like enough? If not, have you in the past, and, if so, why did you stop?

6. Which of your activities contribute to your sense of well-being, sensual pleasure, or artistic expression? What do you do that helps you feel connected with yourself?

7. How much television do you watch on an average day or week? How many hours of video games? How many hours of web surfing? How do you feel after you engage in those activities?

8. Do you feel you have enough time and space in your life? How often do you feel pressured, overly busy, or rushed?

9. Do you consistently take off evenings, weekends, and holidays? If so, what do you do during those times to rejuvenate? If not, why not?

10. How would you describe your current use of alcohol or other recreational substances? In the past? How much caffeine (including chocolate) do you use in a regular day or week?

Now – Circle The Column That Best Describes Your Current Life In This Area.

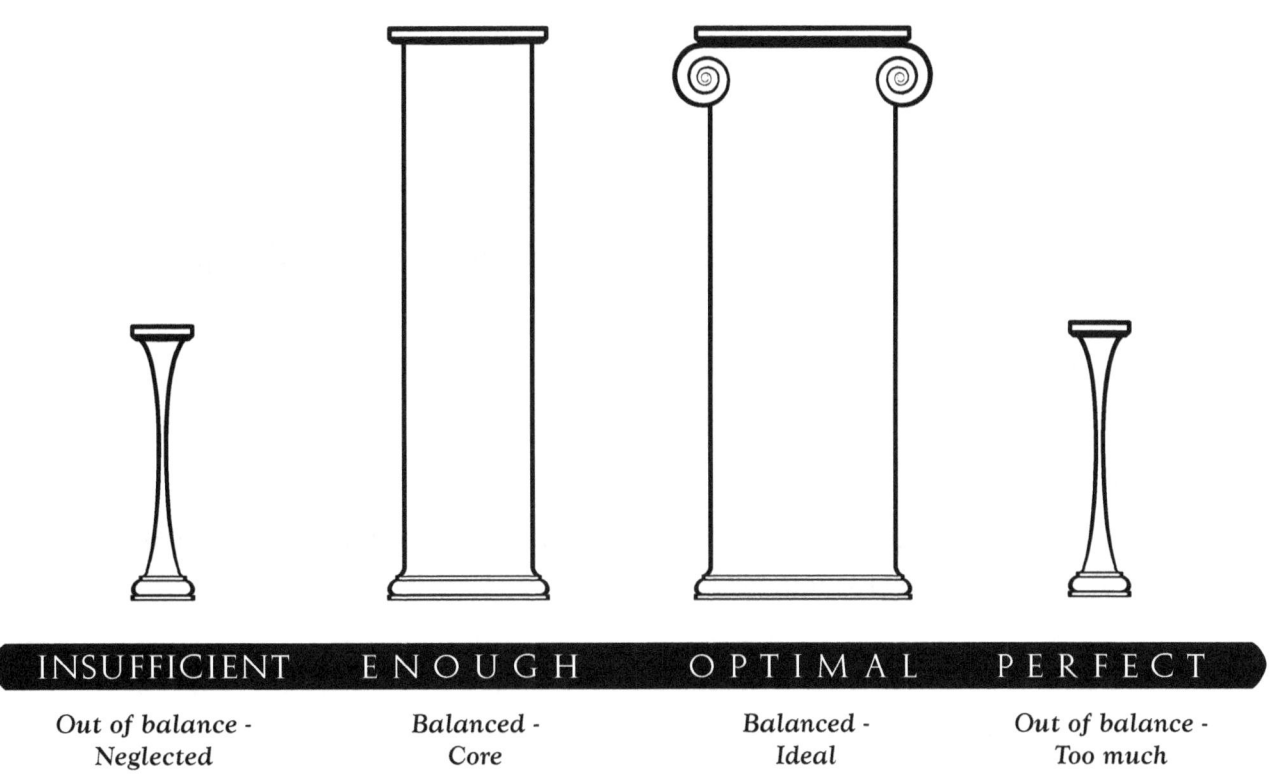

INSUFFICIENT	ENOUGH	OPTIMAL	PERFECT
Out of balance - Neglected	*Balanced - Core*	*Balanced - Ideal*	*Out of balance - Too much*

Movement

INCLUDING BODY IMAGE

Foundation 2 comprises all the ways you are present in your body. This includes movement of any kind, beyond simply exercise and fitness. It includes your feelings about and relationship with your body, as well as your body image.

Answer the questions below about this important area of your life. Take your time and really reflect on your answers.

First Steps

1. How do you feel about "exercise" and "fitness"? Do you tend to feel excited when you think of exercise, or do you get feelings of guilt or "should", or perhaps something else?

2. Do you do any kind of regular exercise? Describe the type and frequency. How do you feel about this routine?

3. Do you consider yourself to be at your ideal body weight? Why or why not?

Going Further

1. Are you basically happy with your body and how you look?

2. How would you describe your physical endurance? Strength? Flexibility?

3. How would you describe your overall physical health? How do you treat any physical or emotional conditions you may have?

4. What kind of movement do you do on a daily or weekly basis?

5. What things in your life do you feel currently have the most effect on your health? Do you feel any of your behaviors contribute to your current state of health?

6. Do you feel empowered to change how your body looks, feels, and functions?

7. Do you have any current fitness goals? Describe any progress you have made on these goals, and any obstacles you have encountered.

8. Do you have any limitations on the kind of movement your body enjoys? How does this affect your daily activities?

9. How often do you miss work due to illness? How often do you work when you are ill?

10. If you imagine yourself in optimal physical health, what would your body feel and look like?

Now - Circle The Column That Best Describes Your Current Life In This Area.

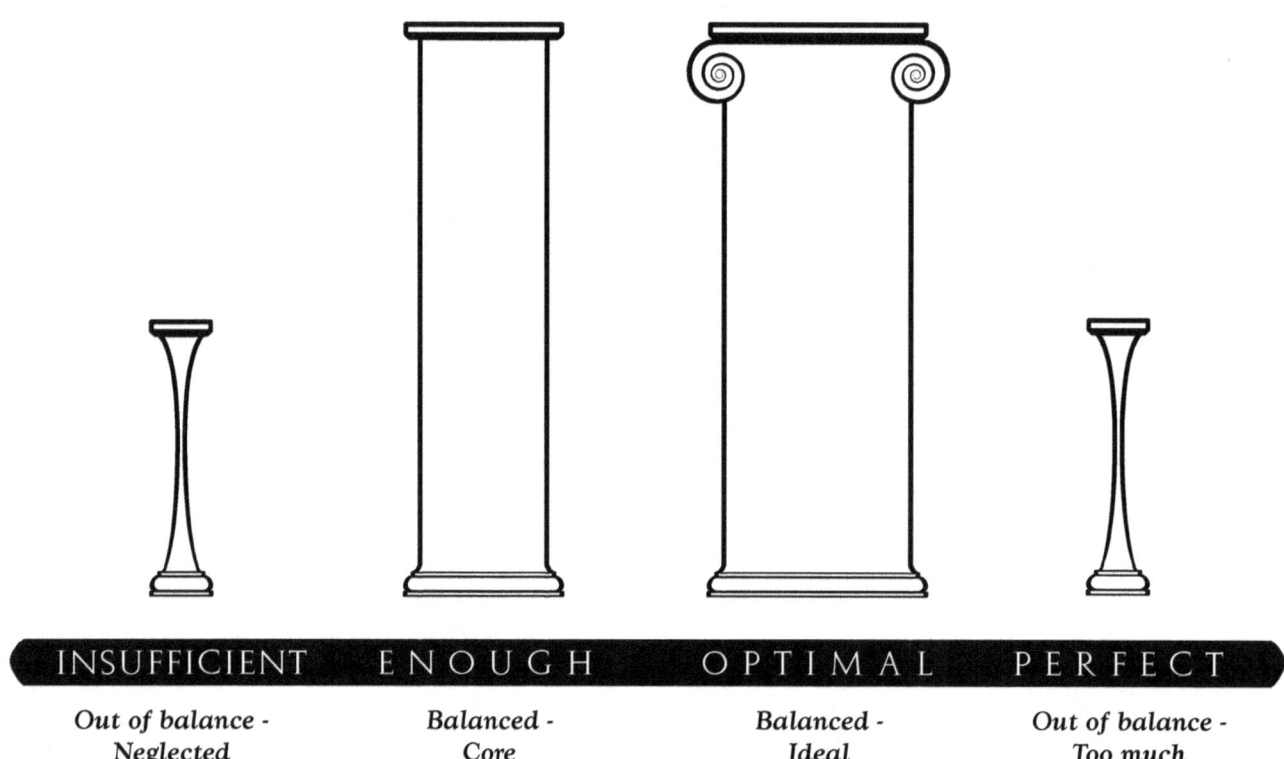

INSUFFICIENT	ENOUGH	OPTIMAL	PERFECT
Out of balance - Neglected	*Balanced - Core*	*Balanced - Ideal*	*Out of balance - Too much*

Nutrition

INCLUDING RELATIONSHIP WITH FOOD

Foundation 3 consists of all the ways you nourish your mind and body. This includes what you choose to eat or not eat, as well as your overall relationship with food.

Answer the questions below about this important area of your life. Take your time and really reflect on your answers.

First Steps

1. How do you feel about your food choices currently? If you could change one thing about your food choices, or do one thing more or less often, what would it be?

2. Do you feel you maintain a healthy diet (low fat, low sugar, high in fresh fruits, whole grains and vegetables)?

3. How often do you "stress eat" or eat for reasons other than hunger?

Going Further

1. How would you describe your relationship with food?

2. Do you have any traditions around eating? i.e. going out to lunch with friends, night snacks with partner, etc.

3. What kind of food do you normally buy, and where do you purchase it?

4. Do you eat meals mindfully, enjoying every bite, or rush through them due to guilt or lack of time, or mechanically without thinking, or to celebrate with those you love, or some other pattern?

5. How do you usually feel after you eat?

6. How often do you eat in your car, in front of the television, or during other activities?

7. Are you able to sense when your body has had enough to eat and stop? Or is portion control a struggle for you?

8. Are you currently on a special diet? If so, please describe it.

9. What is your eating frequency or pattern? How often do you engage in skipping meals, overeating, or binge eating?

10. How often do you eat sugary desserts or salty snack foods? How do you feel before, during, and after eating them?

Now – Circle The Column That Best Describes Your Current Life In This Area.

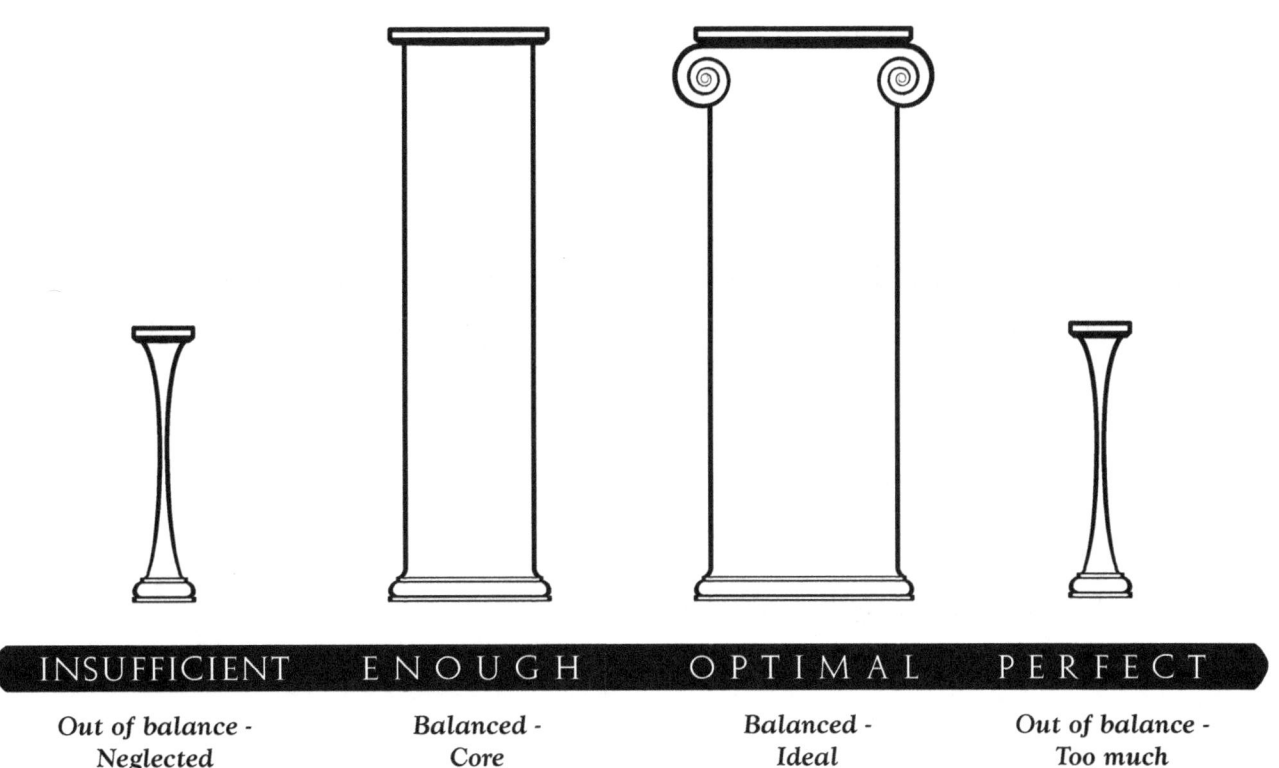

Self

INCLUDING EMOTIONAL/MENTAL, IDENTITY, PERSONAL GROWTH, HISTORY

Foundation 4 embodies all the ways you relate to your true self. This includes your emotional and mental health, your self-identity and self-expression, any personal growth practices, as well as your life history and experiences. Most importantly, though, Foundation 4 is about what truly makes you happy.

Answer the questions below about this important area of your life. Take your time and really reflect on your answers.

First Steps

1. Are you able to fully accept, feel and express both pleasant and painful emotions, including fear, anger, and sadness? If not, why do you think that is? If so, what contributes to your being able to do so?

2. What are your strengths? Your weaknesses?

3. Do the choices you make every day get you what you want? How so, or why not?

4. What was it like for you growing up in your family?

5. If you had a magic wand and could change one thing in your life, what would it be?

Going Further

1. How have you been feeling emotionally lately? Do you feel joy, hope and happiness more or less often than sadness, despair and jealousy? How often do you smile or laugh?

2. What are the first three positive words that come into your mind when you describe yourself? How do you feel as you write these?

3. What are the first three negative words that come into your mind when you describe yourself? How do you feel as you write these?

4. Do you believe it is possible to change? If so, how motivated are you to make productive, healthy changes in your life?

5. How willing are you to take risks or make mistakes in order to reach your goals?

6. Does everything have to be perfect for you to feel satisfied with your performance? What does your "perfect" look like? Do you feel that is attainable?

7. Are you comfortable with and able to make clear requests to let others know what would make you happy? How able are you to make decisions and create boundaries that protect your self-interests?

8. Have you had any events in your life that you consider life-changing or transformative-positive and/or negative? How did these events affect you? How have you responded?

9. Do you look forward to something every day? If not, how often does this happen, and what do you look forward to?

10. Is there anything about your life that you are tolerating or putting up with? What needs is it meeting for you to continue putting up with it?

Now – Circle The Column That Best Describes Your Current Life In This Area.

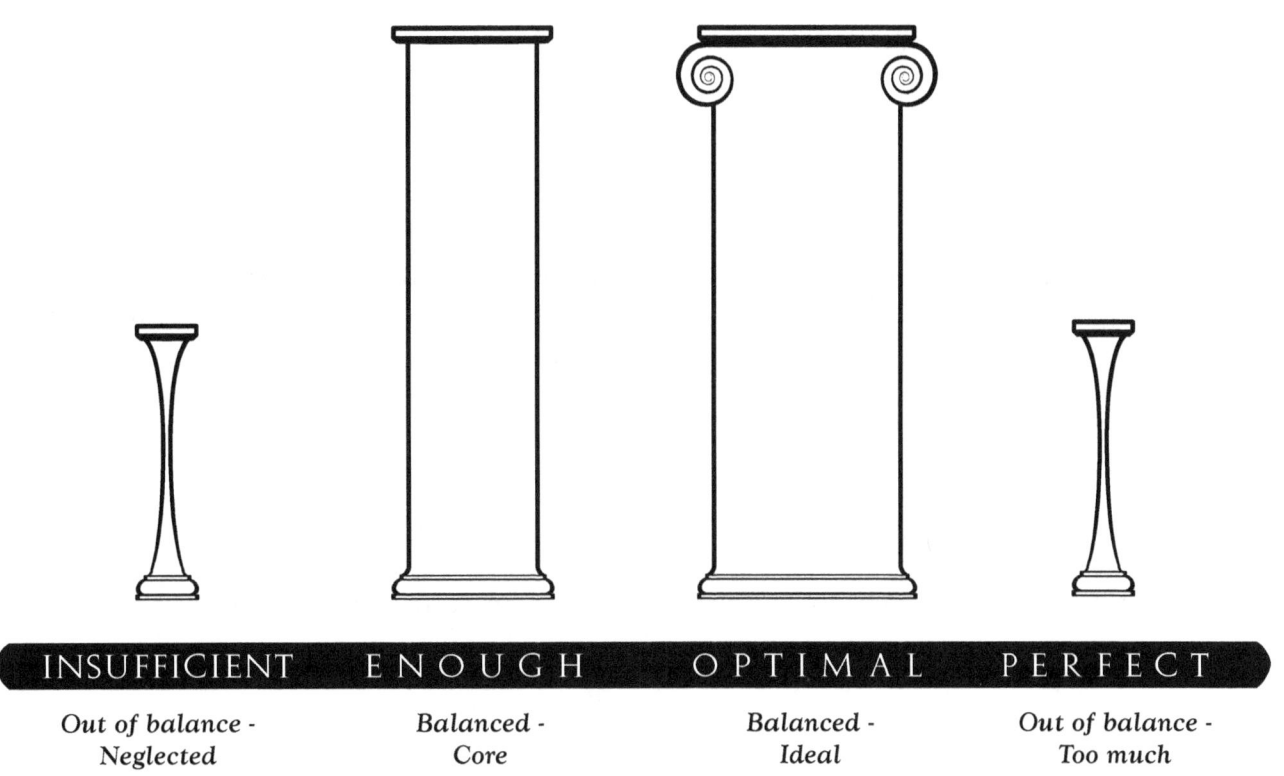

| INSUFFICIENT | ENOUGH | OPTIMAL | PERFECT |

Out of balance - Neglected   *Balanced - Core*   *Balanced - Ideal*   *Out of balance - Too much*

Relationships

INCLUDING COMMUNICATION, TOUCH, FAMILY AND PARTNER, HOME, NEIGHBORHOOD/COMMUNITY

Foundation 5 comprises all the ways you relate to others. This includes how you connect to others you care about, especially communication habits and physical touch, as well as your social environment. Most importantly, though, Foundation 5 is about how you love and receive love.

Answer the questions below about this important area of your life. Take your time and really reflect on your answers.

First Steps

1. Do you have someone in your life with whom you can share everything? Why do you think you connect with this person? If you do not feel you have one right now, what characteristics would such a person need to embody?

2. What forms of touch do you give and receive in your day-to-day life?

3. How would you describe your relationships with your family members? How often do you talk with them?

4. Do you have a strong sense of belonging in your home environment? Do you feel safe there?

5. Do you have a support system of family and friends to assist you in times of need? Can you think of a recent situation in which you received help from others?

Going Further

1. Are you comfortable asking for help? If so, why do you think that is? If not, what do you think stops you?

2. How do you usually handle conflict? Describe a moment of conflict you had in the past week, and how did you handle it?

3. How gratifying are your sexual relationship(s)?

4. What is your romantic relationship(s) like? What about past relationships?

5. Have you forgiven those who have harmed you in the past, whether or not it was intentional? If not, why not, and if so, why did you choose to do this?

6. How have you made amends within relationships that have experienced some pain in the past? Is there anything unresolved with your past loves or spouses? With other past relationships?

7. What relationships provide you the most comfort and connectedness within your immediate family? Which are the hardest to maintain? Why do you think this is?

8. Do you feel a strong connection with and appreciation for your home? Your neighborhood? Your natural environment?

9. Do you have a circle of warm, caring friends? What about this circle contributes to your sense of community, acceptance, and belonging? If not, what would it look like if you did, and what would need to shift to create that?

10. How do you contribute to your larger community? What activities give you the greatest sense of satisfaction?

Now - Circle The Column That Best Describes Your Current Life In This Area.

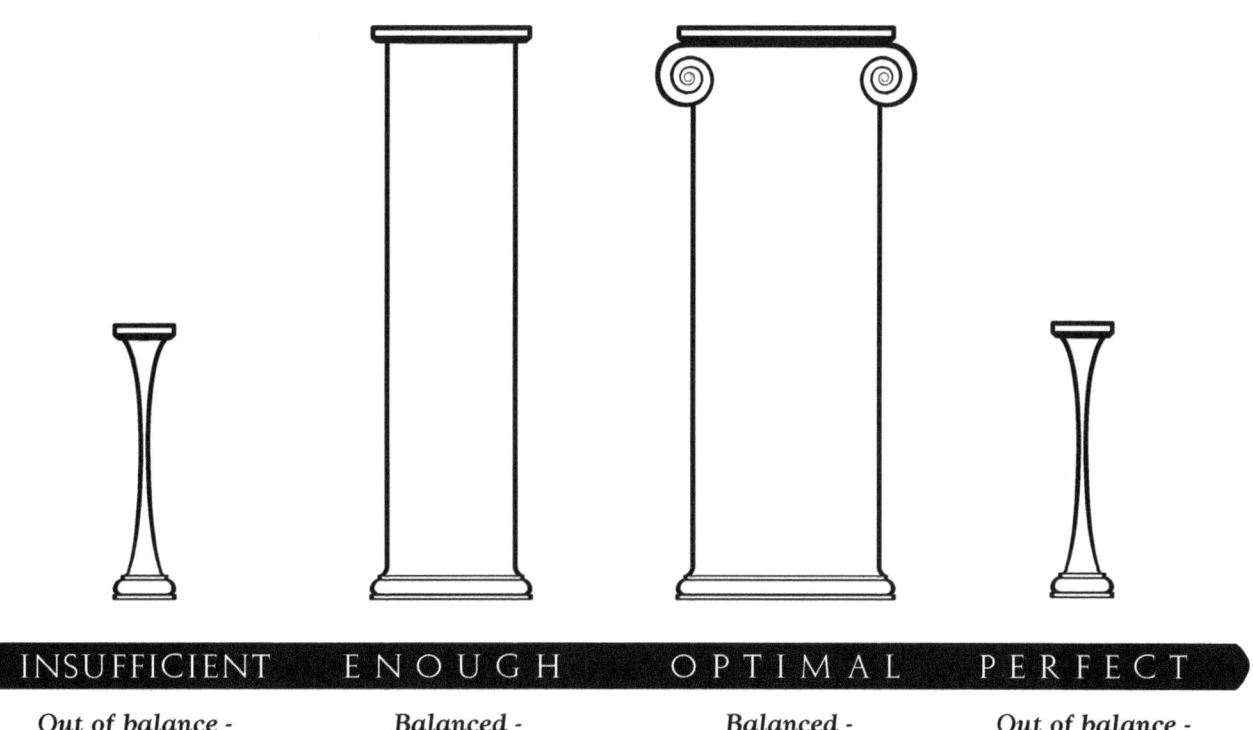

INSUFFICIENT	ENOUGH	OPTIMAL	PERFECT
Out of balance - Neglected	*Balanced - Core*	*Balanced - Ideal*	*Out of balance - Too much*

Work

INCLUDING CAREER (PAID OR UNPAID), FINANCES, WORK ENVIRONMENT

Foundation 6 constitutes all the ways you contribute to the world through your work. The focus here is on your career (paid or unpaid), but it also includes your work environment as well as your financial health.

Answer the questions below about this important area of your life. Take your time and really reflect on your answers.

First Steps

1. What does your work mean to you?

2. How do you meet your financial needs and desires? If all needs are not met, how are you able to make meaningful choices?

3. How are your relationships with others at your work, including both colleagues and supervisors?

Going Further

1. Describe five accomplishments you are most proud of and why.

2. If you were financially able to retire, or otherwise would not need an income one year from today, what would you want your life to look like and what would your goals be?

3. What would you most like to do in the next decade, professionally?

4.   Do you wake up with enthusiasm for the day ahead?

5.   How do you feel about your job? Are you challenged? Are you good at it?

6.   Do you find your work financially and personally rewarding?

7.   How many hours a week do you work? Does this feel like too many? Not enough? Just right?

8. Is money a significant stressor for you? Why do you think this is?

9. Is creating a simpler life a priority for you? Why or why not?

10. Do you feel a sense of acceptance and belonging at work? If yes, why do you think this is? If not, what factors contribute to this situation?

Now – Circle The Column That Best Describes Your Current Life In This Area.

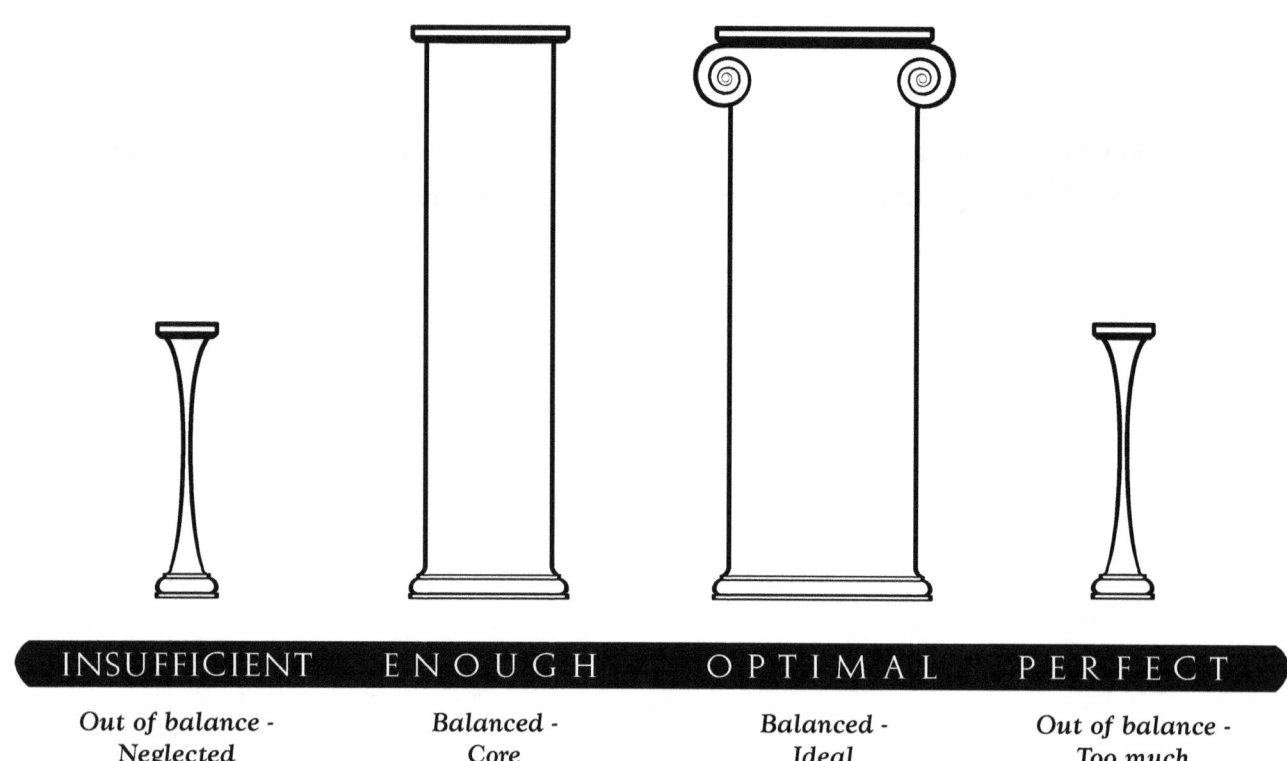

Meaning

INCLUDING SPIRITUALITY AND SERVICE

Foundation 7 embraces all the things that bring purpose to your life. Although true for all the Foundations, it is especially true here that the answers are unique for each person. This Foundation could include spiritual or religious practices, acts of service to others, or simply connection to something greater than yourself.

Answer the questions below about this important area of your life. Take your time and really reflect on your answers.

First Steps

1. Do you have any religious or spiritual beliefs? How important are they to you?

2. Do you feel a higher sense of passion and purpose in your life? If so, how would you describe it?

3. What matters most to you in life? Why are these things important?

4. How do you maintain peace of mind and tranquility?

5. What helps keep you going when times are hard?

Going Further

1. Do you take time for prayer, meditation, or reflection? Where and how does this usually take place?

2. How would you describe the spiritual environment in your childhood home? How do those experiences affect your spiritual understanding or practice now?

3. Is your relationship with God, Spirit, or a Higher Power important in your life? If so, how? If not, describe your personal belief system.

4. What is your greatest hope? For yourself? For loved ones? For the world?

5. What would you most like to do in the next decade, in pursuit of your life purpose?

6. How attuned are you to your intuition? Can you describe a time in the last week or month in which you acted based on your intuition, and what were the results?

7. Is your life enjoyable, rewarding, and fulfilling? If so, why do you think that is? Or if not, why not?

8. What do you get really passionate or enthusiastic about?

9. When do you find yourself so engaged in something that you lose track of time?

10. What brings you joy? For what in your life do you feel gratitude?

Now - Circle The Column That Best Describes Your Current Life In This Area.

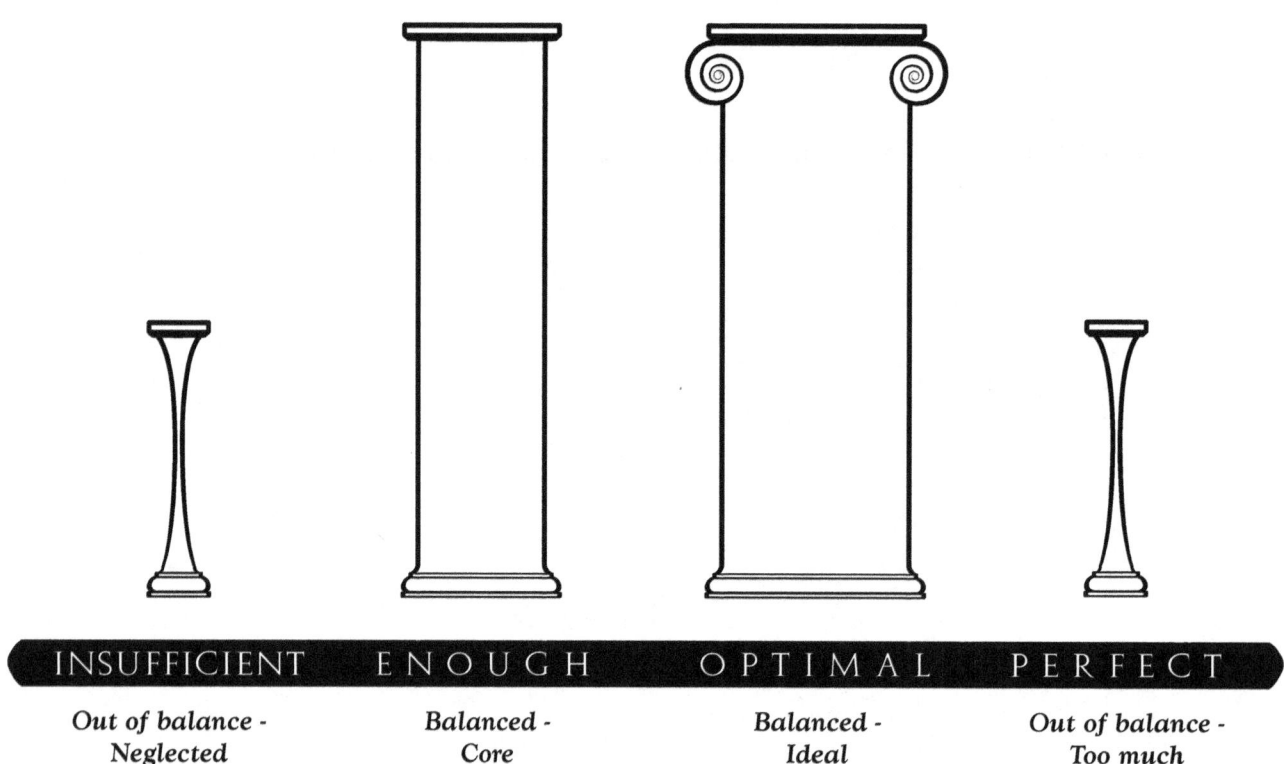

INSUFFICIENT	ENOUGH	OPTIMAL	PERFECT
Out of balance - Neglected	*Balanced - Core*	*Balanced - Ideal*	*Out of balance - Too much*

Building Your Health and Happiness

DO YOU HAVE SOLID FOUNDATIONS?

Building a balanced life requires a solid Foundation in all areas. Gather your column pictures from the preceding 7 sections.

On the following page, color in the column that corresponds to your current life balance in the corresponding area. Then, using a straight line, connect the top of each column to the one next to it.

Now, circle your areas of imbalance.

Look at the patterns you drew on your columns, then take a moment to jot down any insights that may have come to you during this process. Explore the things you wish you were doing, and what might be standing in the way of doing them, but also what things you are doing well and what is supporting you in creating balance in your life.

Notes:

THE 7 FOUNDATIONS OF HEALTH AND HAPPINESS

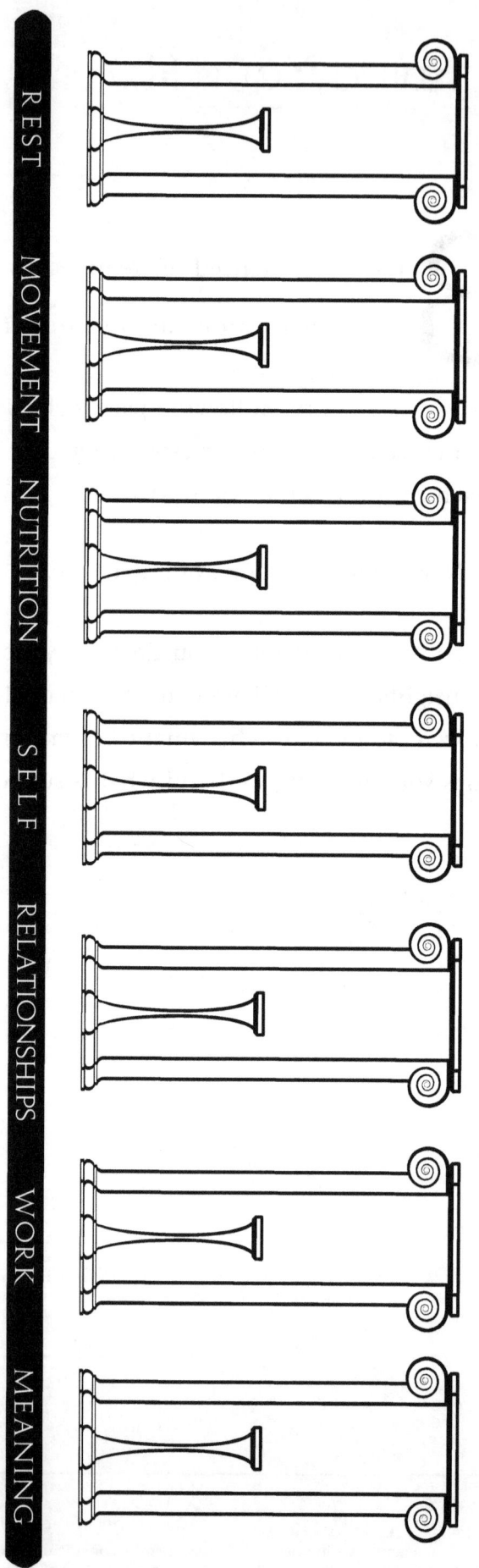

REST | MOVEMENT | NUTRITION | SELF | RELATIONSHIPS | WORK | MEANING

© 2013 Chanel Heermann, SynerGenius Consulting
Denver, Colorado | info@synergeniusconsulting.com | 720-515-1315 | www.synergeniusconsulting.com

BUILDING A CASTLE IN THE SKY?

Just for fun, let's take a moment to imagine your "perfect" life.

On the following page, make a list of everything you think would be involved if you were doing it all "right", just below each column.

Would you be working out 2 hours a day? Meditating for an hour every morning? Spending each evening connecting with your partner over a glass of wine or cup of tea? Just let your imagination run wild and write it all down.

Notes:

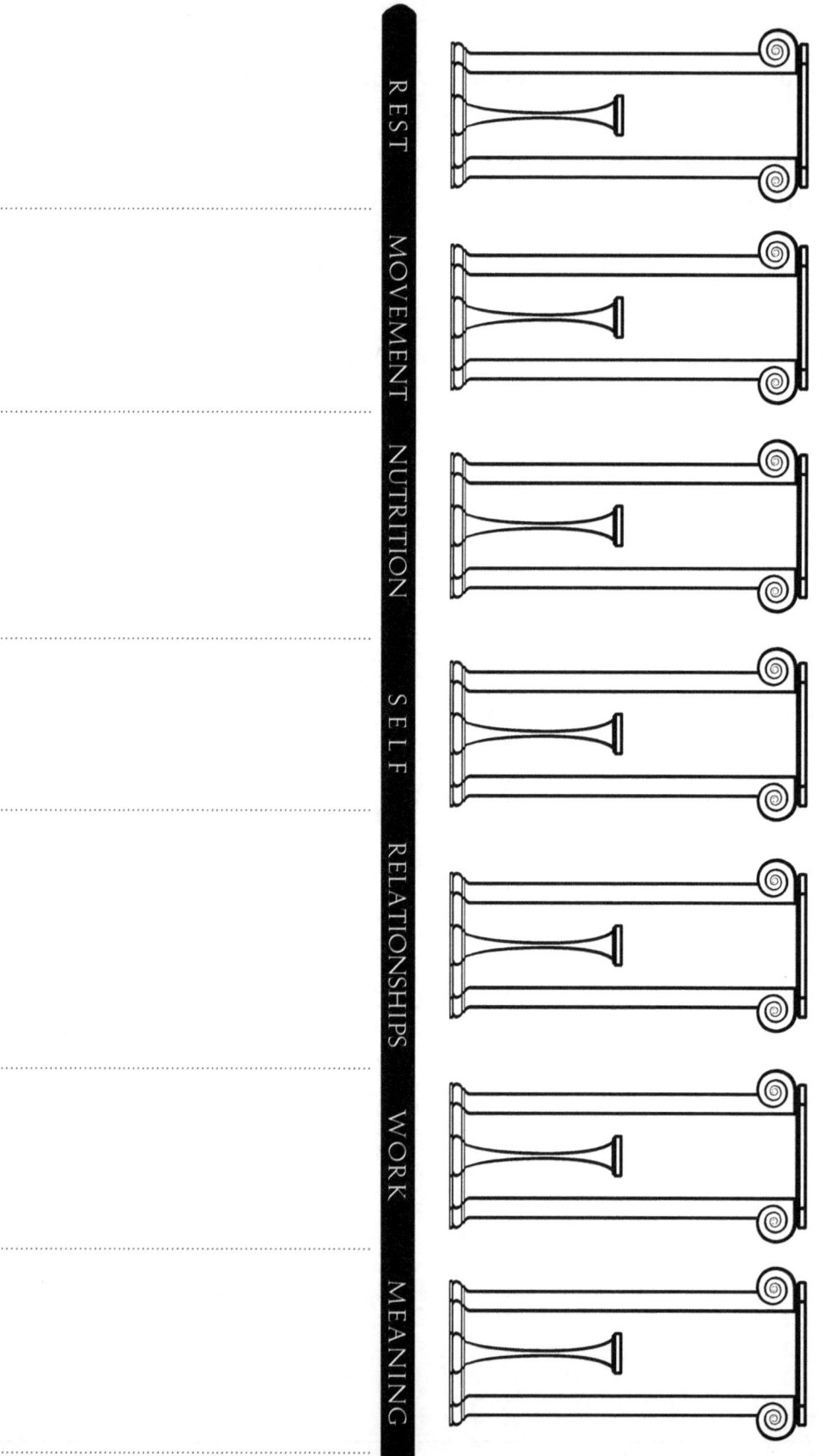

THE 7 FOUNDATIONS OF HEALTH AND HAPPINESS

REST · MOVEMENT · NUTRITION · SELF · RELATIONSHIPS · WORK · MEANING

© 2013 Chanel Heermann, SynerGenius Consulting

Denver, Colorado | info@synergeniusconsulting.com | 720-515-1315 | www.synergeniusconsulting.com

Now take a moment to review what you wrote.

What do you notice as you look over your list? How many hours a day would you need to do all these things?

What would it take to be able to have "perfect" self-care? Would you be able to hold a job? Care for your family? Maintain other responsibilities? Sleep?

Chances are, these are the standards your subconscious mind has been using to compare to your actual performance. Have you noticed that uncomfortable feeling that whatever your doing isn't "enough"? That feeling arises from our unconscious "shoulds" and unrealistic expectations. Unfortunately, our subconscious isn't good at logic, and it's worse at math. You know you only have 24 hours in the day, but all it knows is that you "should" be working out for a certain number of hours or getting a certain number of things done or getting some magic amount of sleep. This sets you up for "failure" every time you don't meet these unrealistic "shoulds". Even if you're not consciously aware of these impossible expectations, they can still drain your everyday happiness.

How would it feel to stop secretly striving for "perfect"?

Instead, take a moment to jot down: what would "optimal" self-care look like?

Notes:

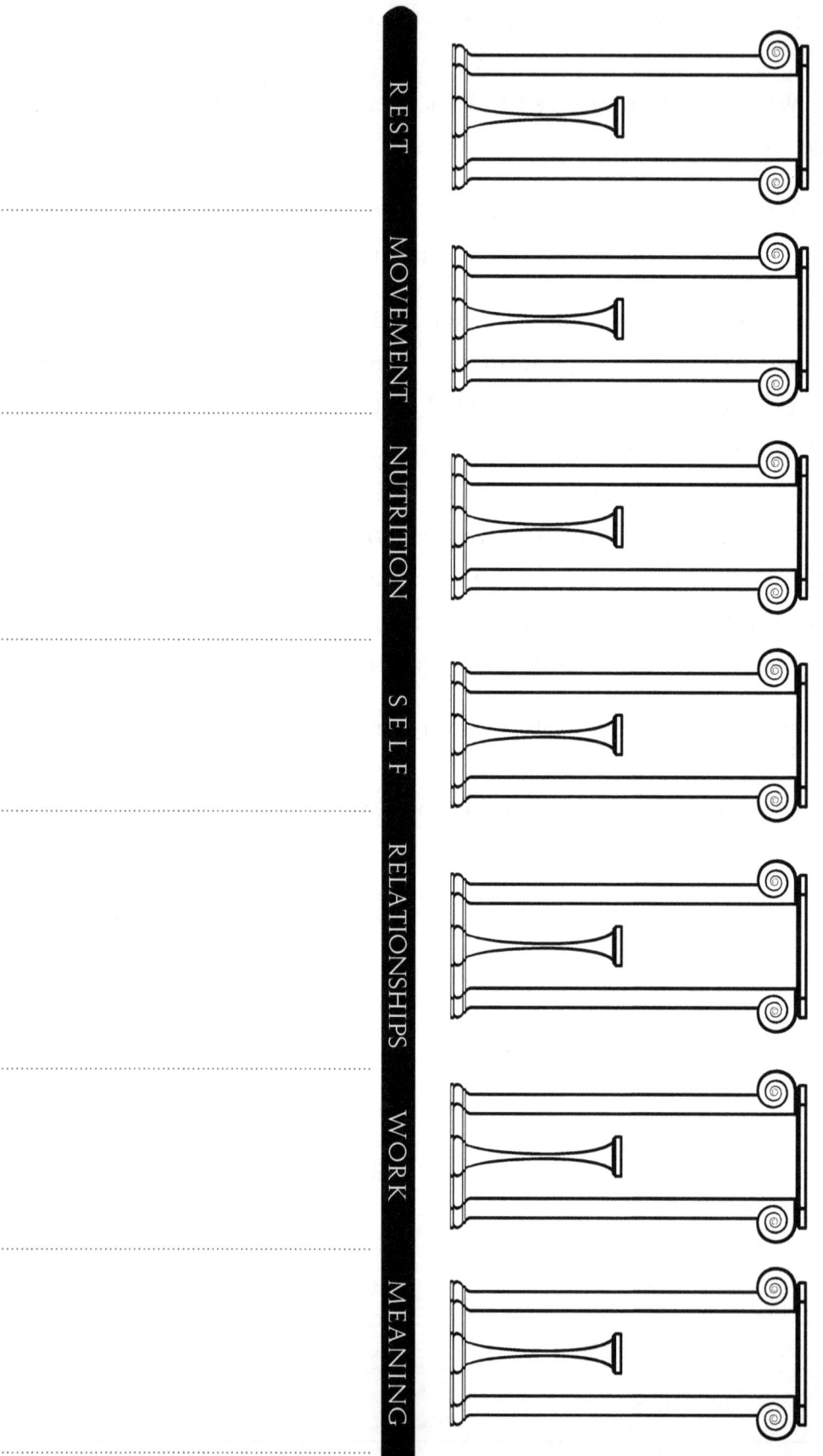

THE 7 FOUNDATIONS OF HEALTH AND HAPPINESS

REST | MOVEMENT | NUTRITION | SELF | RELATIONSHIPS | WORK | MEANING

© 2013 Chanel Heermann, SynerGenius Consulting

Denver, Colorado | info@synergeniusconsulting.com | 720-515-1315 | www.synergeniusconsulting.com

BUILDING A BRIDGE TO BALANCE

Balance is the path to creating a life you love. However, having a good self-care practice doesn't mean that we can "do it all".

The first step to balance is to determine what your "enough" looks like. Sometimes – probably most days – you will have to choose between the hour-long workout, the 8 hours of sleep, and the half-hour of meditation on a given day. That's where the concept of "minimums" or "enough" comes in. Your "enough" is the very least that you can do in the important areas of your life and still continue to nurture and grow those areas. Enough isn't about perfection or even your own personal ideal. It is simply the foundation upon which you can build a life that will support you in becoming the best "you" you can be.

On the following page, make a list of your own personal "enoughs" just below these columns. While you're at it, go ahead and color in the plain, solid columns, and connect their tops, just like you did in the first exercise.

How does it feel to imagine your life being this solid? This balanced?

Notes:

Now, take a moment and look at this new list and the picture above.

Does it feel do-able? Workable? Within reach?

Is there any one thing on this list that jumps out at you? If you had to choose only one, what is the most important thing you could be doing right now to maximize your health and happiness?

Is there one manageable goal you feel moved to set for this upcoming week? If so, write it down below.

Take a moment and write down any further insights, feelings, or thoughts that come up for you as you explore these ideas.

Notes:

NEXT STEPS

Congratulations on completing the most important step in creating your ideal life!

So, now what? Now that you know where you are, where do you go from here, and what is your next step?

GOAL SETTING

In this book, you have been fearlessly examining what you are doing right now, and using that understanding to move past your vague gut feeling that something isn't right and move into action – so you can make a real, lasting change.

So what do you want to do next? I encourage you to take some time now to review your "Building Your Health And Happiness" section. Look over your own "big picture" and think about how your life is now, and how you would like it to be.

You can start creating your ideal life – beginning now. Your first step is to set a goal. It needs to be achievable, both based not only on your own personality and preferences, but also based on the realistic time limits imposed by balancing all seven Foundations, all at once, all the time. Pick something – preferably something small and do-able, but meaningful and important to you. Remember: there is no "right" answer when choosing your next best step. Only you can determine the bottom line for your own personal best life.

This goal needs to be measureable and have a time limit. "I will work out more" is not measureable. "I will work out for 15 minutes 5 days per week for the three weeks" is measureable. The time limit is important. It allows you to have a particular deadline for checking in, evaluating your progress, and making any adjustments needed based on your experience.

Resist the urge to avoid action by doing more research and gathering more information at this stage. Most people already know what to do to improve their lives. They simply aren't doing it. They may be avoiding looking at or be in denial about the ways and whys behind their choices not to implement beneficial changes. Besides, you don't need me, or anyone else, as the "expert" to declare what you "should" be doing. That just replaces your old "shoulds" with a shiny new set of "shoulds". That doesn't begin to accomplish the goal, which is you creating your own ideal life. My wish for you is for your goals to be self-created, based on the science we review together. This process needs to be individualized for you. I want to empower you to create your best life, and not to rely on some "authority" – even me – to decide what fits for you.

TIPS FOR EACH PILLAR

Each Foundation can exist as one of four levels, or Pillars – Insufficient, Enough, Optimal, or Perfect. You probably noticed that I do not distinguish between "Insufficient" and "Perfect". That is because both are equally out of balance. Both are spindly, weak, and an unstable foundation on which to build a life. They only look different in the level of frantic activity and the number of tasks you are trying to complete. But remember: the imbalance you create in your life by doing too much is every bit as destructive as doing nothing at all.

Instead, you want to strive for the "happy medium" – aptly named, since people are happiest when they achieve true balance. In the Pillar system, this "happy medium" is found in either the "Enough" or "Optimal" Pillars. Both of these levels provide a solid, sustainable foundation upon which to build your balanced life. Which Foundations are Enough and which are Optimal will shift over time, depending on your life circumstances. However, the goal is to keep all seven Foundations in that balanced center, regardless of external events, and not to slip into over- or under-doing in any one area.

Flip back through your *7 Foundations to Health and Happiness*, both reviewing the composite pictures with all seven Foundations, and closely reviewing any Foundations that especially stood out for you. Look at where your life balance currently stands in regard to these Foundations. Is your Pillar thin and wobbly? Or strong and stable, able to support your balanced life?

Based on your current status, the pointers below may help you to focus your intentions and set a goal that will make you both happier and healthier.

Insufficient

This is very common, so remember to be kind yourself. The point of this exercise is not self-flagellation about how you "should" be doing better or more. This is key: only try to change one thing at a time. As you read try to narrow this down to your first goal, you will likely notice several areas you feel you could improve on. However, trying to fix them all at once just sets you up for disappointment. You didn't get into this situation overnight, and it won't be fixed overnight – and that is okay.

Enough

Remember the minimum is *okay*! Feel free to move on to another Foundation, or, if you're feeling like you'd like to optimize a little something here or there, read through this guide and choose one change you'd like to make over the next three weeks.

Optimal

If you are already at your optimal level, you would probably be better served by focusing your energy on a different Foundation right now.

Perfect

It is possible to get too much of a good thing in any Foundation. If your self-care routine is so strict that it is keeping you from enjoying your life, it may be time to let something go. If this is you, consider easing up on your current habits, paying close attention to how your body and mind feel during this process.

CHOOSING

After exploring all your options, you may be feeling really stuck, or unable to choose between several worthy goals. A wise mentor once shared this decision-making technique with me for just this case. When you have two options, first start by making a list with two columns — one for each choice. BUT, instead of the usual exercise — writing down pros and cons — just write down the pros, the arguments "for" each choice. The reasoning behind this is that we make the best decisions when they are based on what excites and inspires us. This is the opposite of what we often do — basing decisions on fear or on avoidance of pain, which is what we do when we make a decision based on a desire to avoid the "cons". Instead, if you are coming from a place of enthusiasm — a term that originally meant "divine inspiration" — you will make the very best decision for you. I love this system, both for its effectiveness and for its positivity.

While you're setting this goal, take a moment to sink into it, reflect on it, and imagine how your life would be different if that goal were met. What deep wishes or needs will be fulfilled when you meet your goal? How would that feel for you? How would that affect those you care about?

Take a moment and write down your goal here:

Notes:

ACTION PLANNING

Unfortunately, just having a good goal isn't enough to create a healthy, happy life. Really taking responsibility for your life involves creating a realistic, do-able action plan. This action plan will help you make your goal a reality and maximize your chances for success. Take a few minutes to break down your goal into manageable, bite-sized pieces, and make a list of action steps that will move you on your way. For the previous example, perhaps you need to research a new workout, or find a local yoga studio, or buy a new pair of sneakers? Or maybe you need to locate a reminder app, or an exercise buddy to keep you on track? Make a list of all these little tasks in the order that you will need to complete them. These individual tasks build on one another in a stepwise fashion and add up to achieving your big, important goal.

Also remember, building a life isn't a solo endeavor. Make a list of who could help you meet your goal, how they could help, and when you will reach out to make that request. You may even want to choose someone to team up with to meet the goal together. Most important, imagine how helping you will help them. In our culture, we often put far too much emphasis on independence, to the point that we feel uncomfortable asking for help. But think about it — when was the last time a loved one asked you for help? What was your reaction? Chances are, you may have felt honored to have been asked, enjoyed the connection and closeness of solving a problem together, and enjoyed the satisfaction of contributing positively to someone else's life. Why would you deprive someone of the opportunity to have those same wonderful feelings by contributing to you?

As you know, though, meeting a goal isn't easy. To help boost your resilience to nay-sayers and bumps in the road, make a list of anyone who may actually work against your goal — including yourself. Also, make a list of obstacles that may stand in your way, both obstacles that you have encountered in meeting this goal in the past, and obstacles you can imagine being of concern this time. Notice if you have any negative judgments about yourself — either for past choices or perhaps for not fixing this problem sooner, or maybe negative thoughts about your ability to make that change. Stand back from those criticisms and really look at them — are those thoughts true? In most cases, probably not. Our minds are extremely skilled at self-criticism and doubt, but these doubts are usually not grounded in objective reality. More important, would you say those things to your best friend if they brought this problem to you? If not, take a moment to re-write those judgments so that they are both realistic and compassionate to yourself. Feel free to re-read these encouragements from your own best friend — you! — whenever you feel stuck or discouraged in this process.

Finally, make a list of requests you'd like to make of yourself during this process. Do you need to come up with some strategies for reminding yourself of your goal, such as posting it on the refrigerator, setting an alarm on your phone, writing yourself notes, or asking a friend for help? Having a reminder can be extremely important in whether or not you are successful in moving from a "change" into a "habit". Perhaps what you need from yourself isn't so much memory aids but permission not to be perfect. Do you need a bit more leeway to let up in another Foundation to free up enough energy to achieve this goal? Or maybe, you just need to focus on being gentle with slip-ups, or otherwise compassionate with yourself? Whatever it is, write it down. Remember to be as supportive to yourself as you would be toward any of the helpers you listed above.

Take a moment to reflect on how you are feeling about your new goal. Are you nervous? Doubtful? Reluctant? Then take a bit more time and review the steps above, fill in any gaps, and work through any doubts. Take as much time as you need with this process until you feel ready. You might even want to sleep on it and see if any new insights come to you in the morning. Remember, the most important thing is to set yourself up to succeed. Are you excited and hopeful about your new goal and action plan? Then you're ready to get started!

Notes:

TIPS FOR SUCCESS

No matter where you are right now, the key is to focus on the big picture. Remember: this is not a sprint! You are trying to build a balanced life for the long-haul.

Use these three simple tips to maximize your chances for success:

1. *Your conscious mind can only do one thing at a time.*
   As much as you may love to multi-task, our brains are simply not designed for it. Trying to overhaul your relaxation practice and your exercise habits while cutting out sugar, for example, is likely to overload the circuits, so to speak. Instead, focus on one change this week and see how it goes. Once that change is running on auto-pilot, then you're ready to try something new. However, that may mean focusing on that one high-priority item for a few weeks instead. Overachievers, it's going to be especially hard for you to dial back your urge to do it all at once. But, remember: being selective will maximize your chances for long-term success.

2. *Your decision making ability and willpower decrease with stress.*
   Research shows that stressful tasks dramatically reduce the ability to resist temptation. I'm sure you have noticed the same is true in real life. The less emotional reserve you have, the more likely you are to give into that sweet treat or hitting the snooze one more time. So, if there are outside circumstances in your life that are draining your mental reserve, now might not be the best time to make a major life change. Or, if you choose to go ahead and improve your self-care during a time of high stress, just be aware of these limits and try to be gentle with yourself when you slip.

3. *Habit is more powerful than willpower.*
   One of the most important insights science has given us into behavior change is the power of habit. Whether it's exercise, meditation, or something else new and healthy, the more you can make doing it a "no brainer", the better your chances of sticking with it. Think about it — do you wake up every morning and consider whether you're in the mood to brush your teeth, or go through in your head all

the benefits of tooth brushing? No, of course not — you just brush your teeth, without any thought at all. That's the power of habit, and that's what you want your health behaviors to become. You don't "psyche yourself up" to take a shower, either, and soon your new habits will be running on auto-pilot just like your daily grooming routine. However, new habits will take a bit of energy input at first, so please be patient with yourself.

The second most important bit of common wisdom on behavior change is that it takes three weeks of consistently performing a new behavior for it to become a habit. Pace yourself, and remember it will get easier after the first 21 days. However, that being said, please remember that 21 days is not the finish line. In fact, modern neuroscience indicates that it probably takes 10-12 weeks to create the new neural patterns and connections you need to support your new behavior in becoming a permanent change. Some research even shows that, depending on what you want to change, it can take over 250 days for a new behavior to become truly automatic. Rather than discouraging you from committing to change, my intention in sharing this with you is to encourage you to stick with it, knowing that stutters and trips in your plan are normal and expected.

The most important tip for success, though, is to base any changes you make on compassionate acceptance of where you are right now. You can stay with this gentle acceptance while still focusing on your inspiration to create something that makes you happier. It's hard, if not impossible, to take good care of things we don't value. Value yourself — as you are right this moment — and take good care of you!

Closing

Whatever you learned in this book, whatever goals you selected, and wherever you are in the process of creating your best, happiest, healthiest life, I want to take a moment to say — Congratulations!

This workbook is, indeed, a lot of work. But, I also hope it's been a lot of play ... a lot of learning ... and, most of all, a lot of compassionate connection with yourself.

Wherever you decide to take these new insights, I hope that this process has contributed in some way to your life. I wish you the very best for your health and happiness.

About SynerGenius

SynerGenius was founded by Dr. Heermann to empower individuals to improve their health and happiness by creating harmony in their lives. We provide services via two distinct but complementary sister organizations.

SynerGenius Telepresence offers comprehensive, individualized solutions for improving wellness and overcoming mental health struggles, delivered directly to patients via safe, secure teleconference technology. This is Dr. Heermann's private integrative psychiatry practice, where she helps people combine both conventional and alternative therapies into a holistic, individualized treatment approach for their unique emotional challenges. SynerGenius Telepresence offers a full range of integrative mental health services in several U.S. states - please check the website for the most current availability. Our services include psychotherapy, counseling, medication management, and mental health care for adults.

SynerGenius Consulting provides organizational, group, and individual consulting programs which combine the scientifically proven practices of Mind Body Medicine, Positive Psychology, and Compassionate Communication. They have been carefully developed to guide individuals through the stages of self-assessment, self-acceptance, and self-change. Our unique programs are offered in a variety of supportive formats, designed to work with your busy schedule and developed to fit within any budget. To determine which option would be best for you or your organization, please refer to the "Services" tab on our website for a complete list of our current offerings.

For further information:

Chanel Heermann, MD
SynerGenius

600 17th Street, Suite 2800 South
Denver, Colorado 80202-5428

Phone: 720-515-1315
Fax: 720-528-7755

info@synergeniusconsulting.com

www.synergeniusconsulting.com

REFERENCES

Alex, Janelle. (2013). Retrieved 1/15/13. From http://reconnectwithyoursoul.blogspot.com/2013/01/powerful-questions-to-ground-you.html

American Board of Integrative Holistic Medicine. The Holistic Health and Wellness Questionnaire. Retrieved 8/9/12. From www.wordwendang.com/en/11081/word_496314.doc,

American Holistic Health Association. Wellness from Within: The First Step. www.ahha.org, 1997.

Ben-Shahar, Tal. (2010). Foundations of Positive Psychology, University of Pennsylvania LPS, http://www.sas.upenn.edu/lps/online

Canfield, Russ. THE 360° VIEW. http://www.360medicine.com/pdf/HealthAssessment.pdf, Accessed 8/9/12

Collier, Anne. (2012). Welcome Package Form. Retrieved 10/26/12. From http://www.arudia.com/client-materials.

Craigie, Fred. CAMPS Assessment, Spirituality Module, Arizona Center for Integrative Medicine, Associate Fellowship curriculum, 2005.

Lally, P., van Jaarsveld, C. H. M., Potts, H. W. W. and Wardle, J. (2010), How are habits formed: Modelling habit formation in the real world. Eur. J. Soc. Psychol., 40: 998–1009. doi: 10.1002/ejsp.674

Kashtan, Miki; Lasley, Martha; Beausoleil, François; Kendrick, Gregg; Miyashiro, Marie R. (2011). Making Collaboration Real 2011: Empowering the Workplace. Marshall, California, Marconia Center.

Low Dog, Tieraona. (2012). Love Yourself, Own Your Life video. Retrieved 9/5/2012. From http://www.drlowdog.com/omm-love-yourself.html.

Madden, William. (2008). Personal communication.

Shapiro, Dan. Mind Body Medicine module. Arizona Center for Integrative Medicine, Associate Fellowship curriculum, 2005.